Wind
POWER

T0343970

Rob Waring, *Series Editor*

HEINLE
CENGAGE Learning

Australia • Brazil • Japan • Korea • Mexico • Singapore • Spain • United Kingdom • United States

Words to Know

This story is set in the United States in the state of Iowa [aɪəwə]. It happens in a town called Spirit Lake, which is north of the city of Des Moines [də mɔɪn].

 Energy Past and Present. Read the paragraph. Then match each word or phrase with the correct definition.

Fossil fuels can be used to make energy, but they're bad for the environment and their amounts are limited. In windy places, some people now use wind turbines to make cleaner energy. This energy can be used immediately or sent to an electricity grid and sold. Wind turbines are very tall and have huge wind blades that come together at a hub. These high structures must be set in strong foundations so that they don't fall over.

1. fossil fuel _____	**a.** a system that supplies electrical power to a large area
2. wind turbine _____	**b.** the center of something shaped like a wheel
3. electricity grid _____	**c.** a machine that produces power by using wind
4. blade _____	**d.** a thin, wide part of a machine used to push air or water
5. hub _____	**e.** the hard, solid base that supports a structure
6. foundation _____	**f.** a material that releases heat when it's burned to provide energy

The Fossil Fuels Coal and Oil

pieces of coal

barrels of oil

B **Life in Iowa.** Read the facts about Iowa. Then write the correct form of each underlined word next to the correct definition.

The countryside of Iowa doesn't have many hills so it's very flat.
Farmers in Iowa grow many different crops to eat and sell.
Iowa farmers store winter food for animals in silos.
Some parts of Iowa have strong storms called tornadoes.

1. a large, round building on a farm used to store food and products: _____

2. land that is not in towns or cities and has farms, fields, forests, etc.: _____

3. foods that are grown in large amounts: _____

4. an extremely strong and dangerous wind that blows in a circle and often destroys things as it moves along: _____

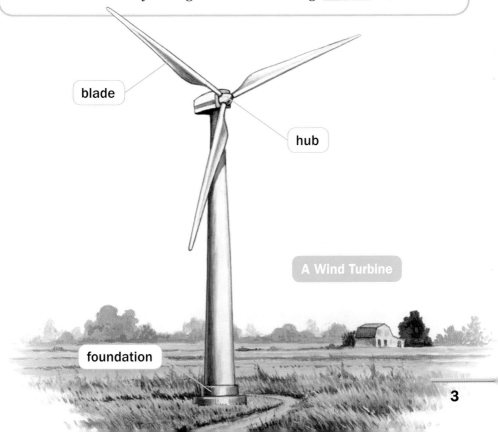

blade

hub

A Wind Turbine

foundation

A round the town of Spirit Lake in the U.S. state of Iowa, the weather is very windy. The land is very flat, and the wind blows across it a lot of the time. For the people who live in the area, it's not always easy to live with the windy weather.

One **school district**,[1] however, is using the wind in order to get an advantage. The school officials in the town of Spirit Lake have built two wind turbines right next to their schools. These turbines are helping the schools to save energy—and money.

------

[1]**school district:** an official area which has a certain number of schools

 CD 3, Track 09

Jim Tirevold, who works with the turbines, explains how much money the turbines have saved the school district. He says: "The little turbine, since it's been **paid off**,[2] has saved the district $81,530." That's quite a bit of money!

Spirit Lake's wind power program began in 1993, when the school district built its first wind turbine. This was the first turbine used to power a school in this part of the United States. Since that time, the school has constructed a second wind turbine. Together, the two turbines could save the district as much as $140,000 a year in energy costs.

---

[2]**paid off:** paid for completely

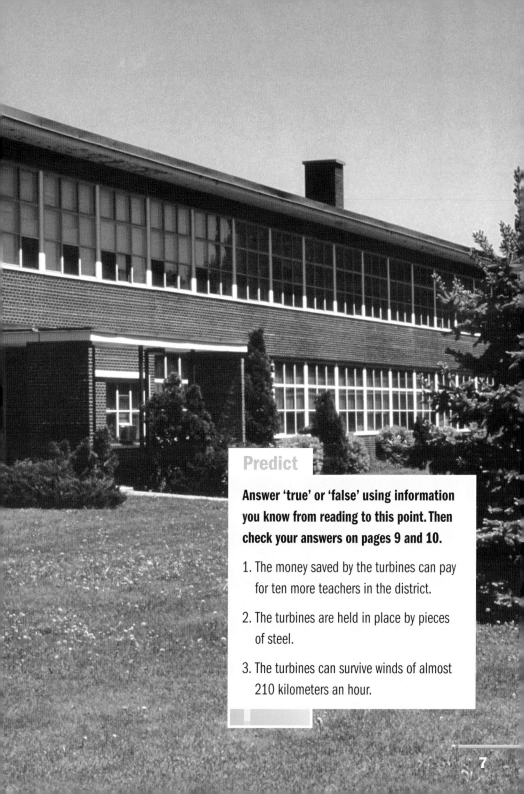

Predict

Answer 'true' or 'false' using information you know from reading to this point. Then check your answers on pages 9 and 10.

1. The money saved by the turbines can pay for ten more teachers in the district.

2. The turbines are held in place by pieces of steel.

3. The turbines can survive winds of almost 210 kilometers an hour.

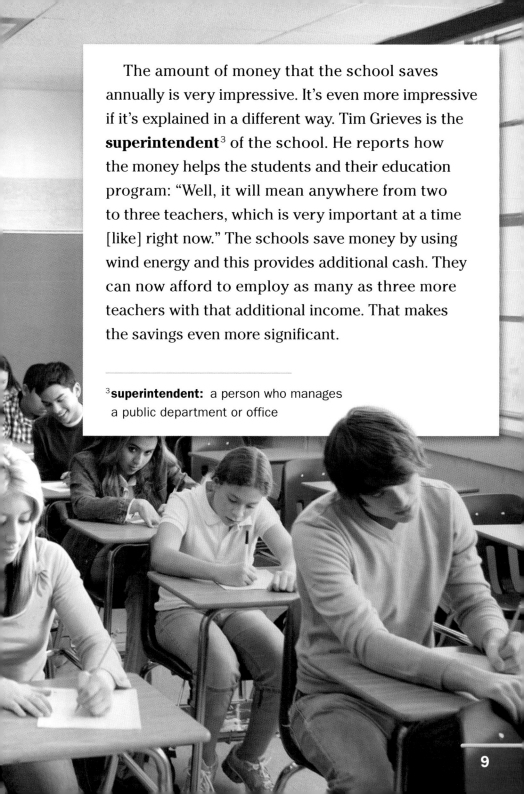

The amount of money that the school saves annually is very impressive. It's even more impressive if it's explained in a different way. Tim Grieves is the **superintendent**[3] of the school. He reports how the money helps the students and their education program: "Well, it will mean anywhere from two to three teachers, which is very important at a time [like] right now." The schools save money by using wind energy and this provides additional cash. They can now afford to employ as many as three more teachers with that additional income. That makes the savings even more significant.

---

[3]**superintendent:** a person who manages a public department or office

But what about the energy-making machines themselves? How are they designed? To understand this, it's best to actually go inside a turbine. From the inside, it's clear just how big the turbines really are. Tirevold takes a visitor into the larger, newer turbine. As the two men look up at the huge structure, Tirevold talks about its size. "This turbine stands 180 **feet**[4] to the hub height," he explains.

The turbine itself is held in place by many steel **rods**.[5] These rods go 25 feet down into a solid foundation. This is done because the wind turbines must be very strong and able to withstand, or survive, very strong winds. But just how strong? "What type of a wind could this withstand?" asks the visitor as he looks around the turbine. "It's rated to stand up to 130 **mile an hour**[6] winds," Tirevold replies. The strength of the turbines is especially important in this part of Iowa, where tornadoes can—and do—occur. In extremely strong winds, the huge blades of the wind turbines are designed to shut down, or stop working.

[4]**feet:** 1 foot = 0.31 meters
[5]**rod:** a narrow piece of material (of metal, wood, or plastic)
[6]**mile(s) an hour:** 1 mile per hour = 1.61 kilometers per hour

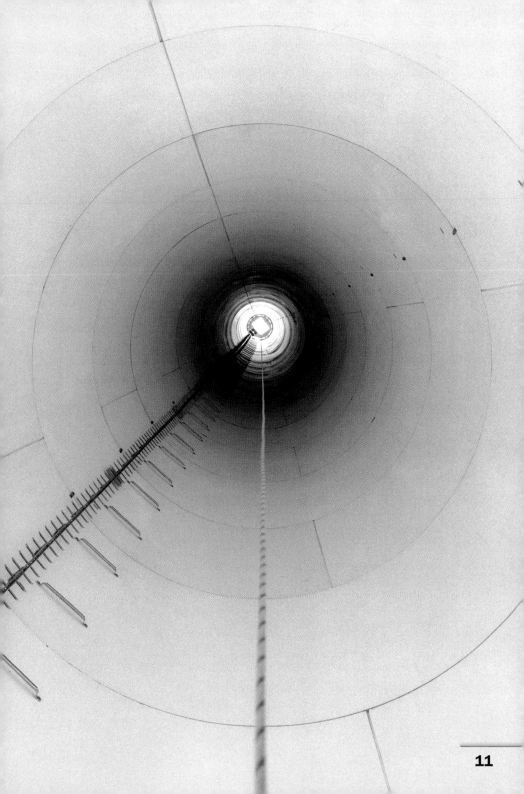

The turbines are also very efficient at using the wind. They are able to produce energy in winds of just eight miles an hour. But what happens to all of this energy? Where does it go?

The smaller of the two turbines at the Spirit Lake School sends its power directly to the school itself. The larger turbine sends its power to the local electricity grid where it can be used by the power company. By doing this, the little school district is able to sell the extra energy that the turbines produce.

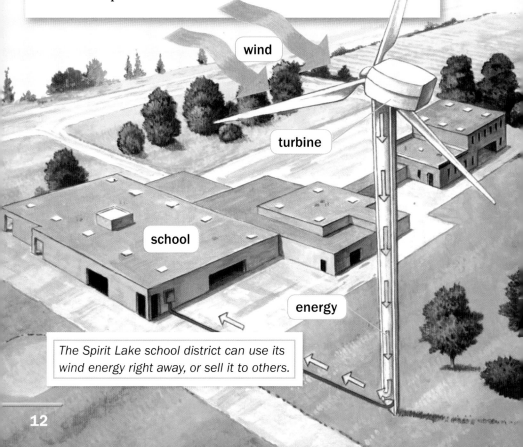

wind

turbine

school

energy

The Spirit Lake school district can use its wind energy right away, or sell it to others.

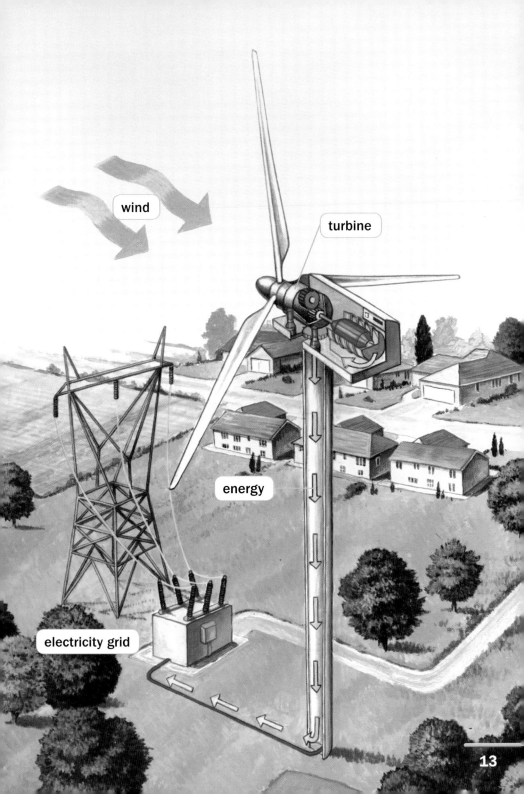

wind

turbine

energy

electricity grid

The schools aren't the only ones who are making money in the energy business. The community around them is also getting involved with wind power production. In the countryside south of the Spirit Lake schools, there are more turbines. They stand near the big silos on local farms. In this area, 65 farmers have recently allowed energy companies to build wind turbines directly next to their fields. Now, the farmers can make money from the wind, just as they do from selling their crops.

Farmer Charles Goodman figures he'll make an extra $6,000 a year from the three turbines on his farm. For him, windy weather means extra money. How does Goodman feel about it? On a visit to the farm, one person decided to find out. "So when you see the wind **kicking pretty good**[7] like it is, that's money in your pocket, right?" asks the visitor. "I smile all the time when the wind's blowing like this," Goodman replies with a little laugh. Wind power seems to be a valuable 'crop' for Spirit Lake's farmers as well.

---

[7]**kicking pretty good:** *(slang)* moving fast

This piece of the Iowa countryside is just 27 miles long, but it now has 257 wind turbines. These turbines provide enough energy to power a city like Des Moines—that's 71,000 homes!

The turbines are also providing more than just power. In the Spirit Lake schools wind power is used for teaching as well. Jan Bolluyt is a **physics**[8] teacher in the school district. He can't imagine why schools wouldn't want to use wind power. He explains: "When I talk [to students] about force, energy, and electricity, they see that we're producing it right here." The wind power program actually provides students with a real-life model of the subjects they are studying in school.

[8]**physics:** the scientific study of natural forces, such as energy, heat, and light

The effects of using a cleaner fuel supply at the school have been impressive. The teachers encourage students to keep detailed records about the wind power program. They write down the amounts of fossil fuels, such as coal, that the school no longer needs for energy. This information clearly indicates that wind power is an alternative form of energy that can be good for the environment. It significantly reduces the production of dirty, dangerous gases that damage the air and the trees. Bolluyt reports how much the program is helping the environment: "We're talking [about reducing] **tons**[9] of **carbon dioxide**.[10] We're talking [about reducing] tons of **sulfur dioxide**.[11] We're talking [about saving] hundreds of trees. So, you know, it's not just a small thing."

In this part of Iowa, people are using wind power to earn money and to learn about saving the environment. The people of Spirit Lake are using the power of the wind to ensure a better future for everyone!

---

[9]**ton:** 1 ton = 907 kilograms
[10]**carbon dioxide:** a gas that is produced when people and animals breathe out (CO_2)
[11]**sulfur dioxide:** a gas with a strong smell (SO_2)

Environmental Benefits of the Spirit Lake Wind Power Program

Carbon Dioxide

2,102 tons

Reduces carbon dioxide by
2,102 tons per year

Sulfur Dioxide

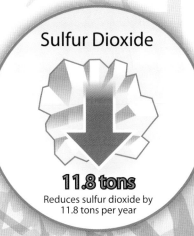

11.8 tons

Reduces sulfur dioxide by
11.8 tons per year

Oil Use

4,000 barrels

Saves over 4,000 barrels
of oil per year

OR

Coal Use

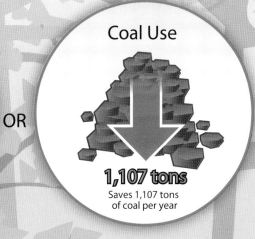

1,107 tons

Saves 1,107 tons
of coal per year

Summarize

Imagine that you are a student at a Spirit Lake
school. Write or talk about the wind power
program and the benefits of wind power.

After You Read

1. The wind blows across Spirit Lake _____ of the time.
   A. all
   B. most
   C. some
   D. enough

2. In paragraph 2 on page 4, the word 'advantage' can be replaced by:
   A. power
   B. support
   C. benefit
   D. help

3. What does Jim Tirevold probably think about the wind turbine?
   A. It's small.
   B. It's expensive.
   C. It's weak.
   D. It's useful.

4. Why did the school build a second turbine?
   A. to get more energy and save more money
   B. because the first turbine wasn't powerful enough
   C. to show the students how to use wind
   D. because they had no electricity

5. On page 9, 'it' in 'it will mean' refers to the:
   A. wind
   B. energy
   C. money
   D. education

6. Which is NOT a good heading for page 9?
   A. School Can Afford More Teachers
   B. Superintendent Excited about Turbine
   C. Money Supports Education
   D. Too Few Students Right Now

7. In extremely high winds, the turbines:
   A. make a lot of energy
   B. turn off
   C. have problems
   D. go slowly

8. What is the purpose of the steel rods?
   A. to hold down the turbines
   B. to withstand heavy rain
   C. to go 130 feet underground
   D. to help the wind get stronger

9. The electricity grid _____ power to be used later.
   A. creates
   B. keeps
   C. designs
   D. survives

10. What is the purpose of page 15?
   A. to show how farmers can earn money from wind power
   B. to show the connection between turbines and silos
   C. to show how wind energy can affect the crops
   D. to show that wind energy makes more money than farming

11. A suitable heading for page 16 is:
   A. Turbines Support School Subjects
   B. Biology Teacher Uses Turbines
   C. School Has Class Outside
   D. Students Love Wind Energy

12. What view is expressed by the teacher on page 18?
   A. Wind is a great fossil fuel.
   B. The school is helping the environment.
   C. Recording data is necessary in science.
   D. The students should plant new trees.

HEINLE Times

TIDAL POWER:
YET ANOTHER ENERGY OPTION

People have been experimenting with alternative ways to make energy for a long time. More than a hundred years ago, people started placing turbines in rivers. The moving water turned the turbine and created power. More recently, companies have begun using the power of the wind to provide electrical energy. Wind farms are now a common sight in many areas of the world. Electricity grids that are connected to these turbines supply electricity to millions of people. Both of these methods avoid the use of fossil fuels and help create a cleaner environment.

Workers lower a tidal power turbine into the East River.

In the past few years, however, there has been increased interest in another energy option on the coasts of the United States. People there now want to use the power of ocean tides, or the rise and fall of ocean water each day. Like wind power, tidal power provides a very clean energy supply. However, it does have one big advantage over wind power. Wind comes and goes and there is no way to control it. Tidal power is predictable and it occurs every day. People who are operating tidal power plants know exactly when the tide will come in and go out.

In some ways, tidal turbines are very similar to those used to make electricity from wind. For example, both types of turbine must have a very heavy foundation. Wind turbines need them because they are very tall and might fall over in high winds. Tidal turbines need them because they are placed in narrow openings on the ocean floor. In these places, the force of the moving water is extremely strong.

In other ways, the two types of turbines are quite different. The blades of a tidal turbine must be much stronger than those of a wind turbine. A company called Verdant Energy learned this lesson quickly. They built some model turbines for its project in New York City's East River. When they put the turbines into the river, the blades immediately broke off from the hub. The company had to design new, stronger blades before the project could continue.

CD 3, Track 10

Word Count: 354
Time: _____

Vocabulary List

blade (2, 3, 10)
carbon dioxide (18, 19)
countryside (3, 15, 16)
crop (3, 15)
electricity grid (2, 12, 13)
feet (10)
fossil fuel (2, 18)
foundation (2, 3, 10)
hub (2, 3, 10)
kicking pretty good (15)
mile an hour (10, 12)
paid off (6)
physics (16)
rod (10)
school district (4, 6, 12, 16)
silo (3, 15)
sulfur dioxide (18, 19)
superintendent (9)
ton (18, 19)
tornado (3, 10)
wind turbine (2, 3, 4, 6, 7, 10, 12, 13, 15, 16)